Very dear Co...

Your Baptism
and to read when you
are older.

With all our love,
Kathy, Rowley & James
x x x

Sunday, 14th September
2008.

to

_____

from

To Amelia, Harriet, Lucie
and Jay A.A.

Written and compiled by Lois Rock
Illustrations copyright © 2003 Alex Ayliffe
This edition copyright © 2003 Lion Hudson

The moral rights of the author and illustrator
have been asserted

A Lion Children's Book
an imprint of
Lion Hudson plc
Wilkinson House, Jordan Hill Road,
Oxford OX2 8DR, England
www.lionhudson.com
ISBN 978-0-7459-4466-1
ISBN 978-0-7459-4843-0 (gift edition)

First edition 2003
5 7 9 10 8 6

Acknowledgments
All unattributed prayers by Lois Rock, copyright © Lion
Hudson, except the Lord's Prayer on page 116. Prayers by
Christina Goodings, Mark Robinson and Sophie Piper copyright
© Lion Hudson. The Lord's Prayer from *Common Worship: Services
and Prayers for the Church of England* (Church House Publishing, 2000)
is copyright © The International Commission on English in the
Liturgy, 1970 and is reproduced by permission of the publishers.

A catalogue record for this book is available
from the British Library

Typeset in 18/28 Baskerville BT
Printed and bound in China

my very first
Prayers

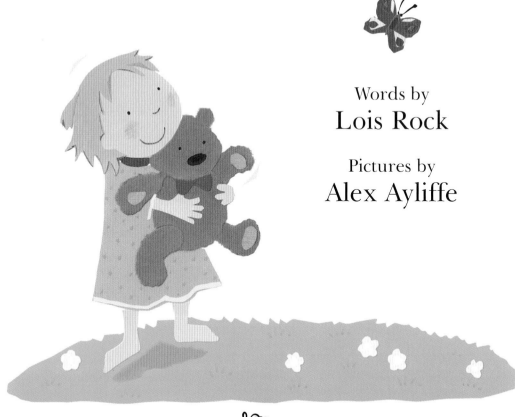

Words by
Lois Rock

Pictures by
Alex Ayliffe

LION
CHILDREN'S

Contents

morning

Dearest God,
on this new day,
listen to me
as I pray.

Dearest God,
the day is new:
help me in
the things I do.

Make all the bedclothes
neat for the day.
Fold the pyjamas,
put them away.
Open the curtains,
look to the light.
May this new day
be filled with delight.

Who made the sun?
Who made the day?
Who made the hours
for work and play?

God made them all,
God made them good,
God helps us live
the way we should.

I wake

I wash

I dress

I say:

'Thank you
God
for this
new day.'

I lift my hands to the golden sun:
A shining day has just begun.
I wave my hand to heaven above:
May God protect me with his love.

O God,
May today be a good day.

May I think something good.
May I say something good.
May I learn something good.
May I make something good.
May I do something good.

May today be a good day,
O God.

This is a day for walking tall
This is a day for feeling small
This is a day for lots of noise
This is a day for quiet toys
This is a day to shout and sing
This is a day for everything.

Dear God,
Your sky is so big
and I am so small.
Never forget me,
never at all.

Dear God,
Please be my special friend:
closer than a hug,
softer than a quilt,
braver than a teddy bear.

Thank you, God in heaven,
For a day begun.
Thank you for the breezes,
Thank you for the sun.
For this time of gladness,
For our work and play,
Thank you, God in heaven,
For another day.

Traditional

me

God, look down from heaven:
Here on earth you'll see
Someone looking upwards –
That someone is me.

Bless my hair and bless my toes
Bless my ears and bless my nose
Bless my eyes and bless each hand
Bless the feet on which I stand
Bless my elbows, bless each knee:
God bless every part of me.

I look in the mirror and what do I see?
Someone who looks exactly like me!
I go out exploring but I haven't met
Anyone even a bit like me yet.

Dear God,
They say everyone's special,
As special as special can be.
But inside I just feel normal –
Is everyone special but me?

Dear God,

There is only one me.

I like what I like.

I don't like what I don't like.

I think what I think.

I do what I do.

I'm the only one of me you've got.

Please take care of me.

Happy, sulky, smiling, sad
Often good and sometimes bad
Through these ever-changing moods
Help me, God, to grow up good.

Dear God,

Please love me when I've been good.

Please love me when I've been bad.

Please love me when I've been ordinary.

Dear God,
Please help me to be really me
when I am with my family.

Help me to be really me
when I am with my friends.

Help me to be really me
when I am all by myself.

Dear God,

Some people forget my name.

Some people muddle my name.

Please will you remember my name

And remember me.

God, who made the earth,
The air, the sky, the sea,
Who gave the light its birth,
Careth for me.

God, who made the grass,
The flower, the fruit, the tree,
The day and night to pass,
Careth for me.

Sarah Betts Rhodes

people
I love

God bless all those that I love;
God bless all those that love me;
God bless all those that love those
that I love,
And all those that love those that
love me.

New England sampler

Dear God,

When my mum is happy,

Let us laugh and play together.

When my mum is busy,

Let us do the work together.

When my mum is worried,
Let us sort things out together.

When my mum is weary,
Let us sit and rest together.

Dear God,
May my dad grow stronger and
wiser and funnier and cleverer.

Dear God,
May my mum grow stronger and
wiser and funnier and cleverer.

Dear God,
When I am with my mum and dad,
help me to take care of them.

When I am not with my mum and dad,
please take care of them for me
and bring us safely together again.

Grans are good
and grans are fun.
Let us love them –
every one.

God bless Grandad
through the bright blue day.
God bless Grandad
through the dark grey night.
God bless Grandad
when we hug together.
God bless Grandad
when we're out of sight.

I say a prayer for Baby –
'God help you and God bless,
God guard you and God guide you
With love and gentleness.'

Dear God,
Please love me
Love my sister
Love my brother.

Dear God,
Please take care of me
Take care of my sister
Take care of my brother.

Dear God,
Please bless me
Bless my sister
Bless my brother.

Thank you, dear God,
for the many kind people
who help us along our way,
who smile when we're happy,
who care when we're tearful,
who keep us safe all through the day.

Dear God,
Help me to be kind and gentle, friendly
and respectful to everyone I meet.

at home

Bless the window
Bless the door
Bless the ceiling
Bless the floor
Bless this place which is our home
Bless us as we go and come.

When the weather is cold
May our home be warm.

When the weather is wet
May our home be dry.

When the sun shines hot
May our home give shade.

When the world is dark
May our home be bright.

Let us take a moment
To thank God for our food,
For friends around the table
And everything that's good.

Knife and fork
and plate and spoon –
May the meal
be here soon.

Spoon and plate
and fork and knife –
Thank you, God,
who gives us life.

The Lord is good to me,
And so I thank the Lord
For giving me the things I need,
The sun, the rain, the appleseed.
The Lord is good to me.

Attributed to John Chapman,
planter of orchards

For health and strength
and daily food,
we praise your name,
O Lord.

Traditional

Underwear everywhere
Shoes in twos
So many clothes
I just can't choose.

So many clothes
I know I'm blessed
But oh – it's so hard
To get dressed.

The room is almost tidy
The toys are put away
I take a quiet moment
To thank God for the day.

Thank you, God, for all things cuddly
In a heap that's soft and muddly
Where I can lie down and rest
Like a dormouse in its nest.

things
I do

God, can you hear me?
This is my prayer:
Please take good care of me
Everywhere.

Dear God,
Teach me to be patient
so I can learn new things
one step at a time.

Dear God,

I think I've learned to walk,

Please help me learn to run,

And can you teach me somersaults?

They look like so much fun.

May my hands be helping hands
For all that must be done
That fetch and carry, lift and hold
And make the hard jobs fun.

May my hands be clever hands
In all I make and do
With sand and dough and clay and things
With paper, paint and glue.

May my hands be gentle hands
And may I never dare
To poke and prod and hurt and harm
But touch with love and care.

Words can make us happy
Words can make us sad
Words can leave us feeling calm
WORDS CAN MAKE US MAD!
So we must be careful
In the things we say
Dear God, help us choose the words
That we use today.

Let us build our friendships carefully
And if we should fall out and argue
Let us build our friendships carefully again.

Dear God,
Please help me learn to say, 'I'm sorry.'
Please help me learn to say, 'I forgive.'

When I am in a temper
When I get really mad
I can be very dangerous
I can be very bad.

I'm wild as a tiger
I'm wild as a bear
I'm wilder than a wildebeest
And I don't even care.

Dear God, who made the tiger,
Dear God, who made the bear,
Please let me know you love me still
And that you'll always care.

Mark Robinson

We give thanks
for all the things that are our very own.

We give thanks
for all the things that are ours to share.

We give thanks
for all the things that others share with us.

We give thanks
for all the things we can enjoy together.

God take care of everyone
Until we meet again
Keep us safe through sun and snow
And wind and hail and rain.

Out and about
And feeling small
God, please help me
If I fall.

Out and about
And walking tall
Trusting God
Not scared at all.

May God be watching over us
when we go out bravely.
May God be watching over us
so we come back safely.

all the animals

All things bright and beautiful,
All creatures great and small,
All things wise and wonderful,
The Lord God made them all.

Mrs C.F. Alexander

The little bugs that scurry,
The little beasts that creep
Among the grasses and the weeds
And where the leaves are deep:
All of them were made by God

As part of God's design.
Remember that the world is theirs,
Not only yours and mine.

Dear God,
Please show extra kindness and love
to worms and snails and snakes and
frogs and everything strange and
slimy. Help us not to frighten them
even if they frighten us.

May the creatures of the wood
Live together as they should.

Dear Father, hear and bless
Thy beasts and singing birds,
And guard with tenderness
Small things that have no words.

Traditional

Dear God,
Thank you for the farmers
who work so hard to keep
their animals healthy and happy.

Dear God,
We hear cows mooing
and are glad for the milk they give us.

We hear sheep bleating
and are glad for the wool they give us.

We hear hens clucking
and are glad for the eggs they give us.

We hear all the sounds of the farmyard
and give thanks for the animals.

Bless the hungry lion and its ROAR

Bless the big brown bear and its GROWL

Bless the sly hyena and its scary HA HA HA

Bless the wolves who see the moon and HOWL!

Multicoloured animals
With stripes and dots and patches:
God made each one different –
There isn't one that matches.

Dear God,
May our dog be loyal and
obedient and patient and gentle
and kind and fun. May everyone
in the family learn to be like that.

Dear God,

Please bless the cat.

Make it wild enough to be a great explorer.

Make it tame enough to come back home.

When little creatures die
And it's time to say goodbye
To a bright-eyed furry friend,
We know that God above
Will remember them with love:
A love that will never end.

If you have heard
the sound of birdsong
in the morning air,
then you will know
that heaven's music
reaches everywhere.

great
big world

Planet home,
our planet earth:
you have cradled us from birth.

Planet earth,
our planet home:
you were made by God alone.

Thank you, dear God,

For the good earth:
I stand upon it.

For the clean air:
I can breathe it.

For the pure water:
I can drink it.

For the fiery sun:
It warms the good earth.

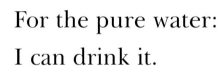

Sunrise, moonrise,
Day and night:
Thank you, God,
For dark and light.

O God,

Keep the oceans and the seas
    where they belong,
Keep the rains and rivers
    where they belong,
Keep the highlands and the
    lowlands where they belong,
So that all your creatures may have
    a safe place to make their home.

Lord of the ocean,
Lord of the sea:
Let the fish swim
Strong and free.

Lord of the wavetops,
Lord of the shore:
Keep them safe
For evermore.

The trees grow down,
down into the earth,
right down into long ago.

The trees grow up,
up into the sky,
right up where the strong winds blow.

The trees, they sway,
they sway in the wind
and whisper a secret song:

'We thank you, God,
for keeping us safe,
that we might grow tall and strong.'

For sun
and for showers,
for seeds
and for flowers,
we give you thanks,
O God.

Angels spend the sunshine hours
Opening the summer flowers.
At the coming of the night
They come back to close them tight.

The morning clouds are orange and pink
As the sun climbs into the sky,
And white clouds drift in the faraway blue
At noon when the sun is high.
The sunset mixes up purple and mauve
With violet, gold and red,
And angels watch over me through the dark
When I'm asleep in my bed.

around
the year

May the rain fall softly:
no flooding.
May the wind blow gently:
no storm.
May the sun shine brightly:
no burning.
May the weather be kindly
and warm.

God is waking the world again
Cold and frost are going.

God is waking the world again
New green leaves are growing.

God is waking the world again
Warmer winds are blowing.

God is waking the world again
Springtime flowers are showing.

Yesterday
I liked the rain,
But, dear God,
Please, not again!

Out of doors in the summer
Out of doors in the sun
Thank you, God, for the summer
And all of our outdoor fun.

A summertime place
of trees and flowers,
the gentle call of a dove,
the hum of a bee –
these things must be
a glimpse of heaven above.

Autumn berries
round and red:
by God's hand
the birds are fed.

Grey cloud, send your rain
to the green and growing grain.
White cloud, blow away
from the golden harvest day.

Winter boots for puddles
Winter boots for snow
Winter boots for all the muddy
  places that I go.

Winter hats for chilly days
Winter hats for storms
Thank you, God, for winter clothes
  that help to keep us warm.

The winter trees
are grey and bare.
God gives them
silver frost to wear.

Spring is green and yellow
and the summer, pink and gold.
Autumn's red soon turns to brown –
the year is getting old.
Wintertime is blue and white –
the ice is crystal clear:
All the colours dance around
the circle of the year.

quiet
times

I'm standing here upon the earth
and looking to the sky.
I'm trusting that my quiet prayers
can reach to God on high.

Dear God,

Are you very grand?

Are you very holy?

Am I allowed to come near?

For I am not at all grand.

I don't really understand holy.

But I feel your love all around me.

Dear God,
Help me to grow up good,
and show me the way I
should go, so that I may
come at last to heaven and
already feel at home there.

I'm sitting
and thinking
and wondering
and wishing
and dreaming
and hoping
and praying

and hoping
and dreaming
and truly
believing
that God
can hear all
that I'm saying.

Dear God,
I am asking in my prayers:
May I receive all you want to give me.

Dear God,
I am seeking for you in my life:
May I find you and learn how to live
as your friend.

Dear God,
I am knocking on the door of heaven:
Open the door to your heavenly
home, where I may live as your
friend for ever.

Based on Matthew, chapter 7, verses 7–8

Dear God,
Please hear my prayers,
even when I cannot think
of the right words to say.

Dear God,
I am a brave explorer
in the world you have made.
Help me to make great discoveries
and to grow wise.

Dear God,
Everything I see in the world tells
me that there must be a Maker,
and I believe that Maker is you.

Our Father in heaven,
hallowed be your name,
your kingdom come,
your will be done,
on earth as in heaven.
Give us today our daily bread.
Forgive us our sins
as we forgive those who sin against us.
Lead us not into temptation
but deliver us from evil.
For the kingdom, the power,
and the glory are yours
now and for ever.
Amen.

make everything better

Dear God, I believe in goodness:
I believe it is stronger than badness.

Dear God, I believe in happiness:
I believe it is stronger than sadness.

Dear God,
May your good world
take care of us.
May we take care
of your good world.

Dear God,
When a perfect day
is spoiled,
help us find a way
to mend it.

Deeply gloomy
Deeply sad
When the day
Goes deeply bad.

Deeply hoping
God above
Will enfold me
In his love.

We say goodbye,
knowing that God loves me
and God loves you.

We say goodbye,
knowing that God will remember me
and God will remember you.

We say goodbye,
knowing that God will take care of me
and God will take care of you.

Dear God,
When things end in tears,
give us joyful beginnings.

Dear God,
I am feeling poorly –
wrap me in softness.

Dear God,
I am feeling poorly –
wrap me in cosiness.

Dear God,
I am feeling poorly –
wrap me in sleepiness.

Dear God,
Let me feel sleepy
and dream in happiness.

Dear God,
We think of those who are sick
and ask you to make them well.

Whenever there's something to share,
Help me to learn to be fair.

Heal the world's sorrows
Dry the world's tears
Calm the world's worries
End the world's fears.

Dear God,
May all the children of the world
have all they need
to grow up well
and to grow up happy.

special days

For each new year
and all it brings,
we give you thanks,
O God.

I count the days to Christmas
and I watch the evening sky.
I want to see the angels
as to Bethlehem they fly.

I'm watching for the wise men
and the royal shining star.
Please may I travel with them?
Is the stable very far?

I count the days to Christmas
as we shop and bake and clean.
The lights and tinsel sparkle,
and yet deep inside I dream

that as we tell the story
of Lord Jesus and his birth,
the things of everyday will fade
as heaven comes to earth.

A prayer for Advent

Away in a manger, no crib for a bed,

The little Lord Jesus laid down his sweet head.

The stars in the bright sky looked down where he lay,

The little Lord Jesus asleep on the hay.

The cattle are lowing, the baby awakes,

But little Lord Jesus, no crying he makes.

I love thee, Lord Jesus! Look down from the sky,

And stay by my side until morning is nigh.

Be near me, Lord Jesus, I ask thee to stay

Close by me for ever, and love me, I pray.

Bless all the dear children in thy tender care,

And fit us for heaven, to live with thee there.

A traditional Christmas carol

There is a green hill far away,
Outside a city wall,
Where the dear Lord was crucified
Who died to save us all.

He died that we might be forgiven,
He died to make us good;
That we might go at last to heaven,
Saved by his precious blood.

A traditional Good Friday song with
words by Mrs C.F. Alexander

In the Easter garden
the leaves are turning green;
in the Easter garden
the risen Lord is seen.

In the Easter garden
we know that God above
brings us all to heaven
through Jesus and his love.

Seed and shoot and ear and grain
Growing in the sun and rain.
Grain and flour and dough and bread –
By God's harvest we are fed.

A harvest prayer

The apple-tree blossom was pink and white
The summertime fruits were green
But now the apples of red and gold
Are much too much for the tree to hold:
God's harvest blessings are seen.

A harvest prayer

Dear God,
When the darkness makes us feel
afraid, bring us safely into the
light of your goodness and love.

A prayer for All Saints' Eve

Dear God,
We think of the people
we know today
who help us
to follow Jesus.

We think of the people
from days gone by
whose stories help us
to follow Jesus.

We think of their wise words
and their good deeds
and ask you to help us
to follow Jesus.

A prayer for All Saints' Day

Tucked up in my little bed,
I say a little prayer
For all the people in this house
And people everywhere.

Sophie Piper

Hands together, close your eyes,
Pray to God above
That the night be filled with peace,
And the day with love.

Sophie Piper

Now I lay me down to sleep,
I pray thee, Lord, thy child to keep;
Thy love to guard me through the night
And wake me in the morning light.

Traditional

Jesus, friend of little children,
Be a friend to me;
Take my hand and ever keep me
Close to thee.

Walter J. Mathams

Kindly Jesus, lead me
as a shepherd leads the sheep
to the greenest pastures
and the quiet waters deep.
Guard me from all dangers
and the fear that haunts the night.
In your goodness, bring me safely
into heaven's light.

The moon shines bright,
The stars give light
Before the break of day;
God bless you all,
Both great and small,
And send a joyful day.

Traditional

I see the moon,

And the moon sees me:

God bless the moon,

And God bless me.

Traditional

The angel of dreams
   is dressed in blue –
A dream for me
   and a dream for you.

The angel of dreams
   is dressed in pink –
And softly into
   your bed you sink.

The angel of dreams
   is dressed in white –
The day is done
   and so goodnight.

Sophie Piper

Clouds in the sky above,
Waves on the sea,
Angels up in heaven
Watching over you and me.

Christina Goodings

Close your eyes,
And safely sleep,
Heavenly angels
Watch will keep.

Sophie Piper

first lines